We Love Holidays
CHRISTMAS

Saviour Pirotta

PowerKiDS press.

New York

Saviour Pirotta is a highly experienced author, who has written many booksfor young children. He was born in Malta and is also a trained chef.

Published in 2008 by The Rosen Publishing Group, Inc.
29 East 21st Street, New York, NY 10010

First Edition

The publishers would like to thank the following for allowing us to reproduce their pictures in this book:

Corbis: 5, Ariel Skelley; 6, Sandro Vanini, Ottaviano di Martino Nelli; 8, David Mercado; 10, Pagani Flavio, Corbis Sygma; 12, Adam Woolfitt; 13, Ted Spiegel; 15, Lucy Pemoni; 16, 18, Becky Lulgart-Stayner; 19, Joseph Sohm; 20, Mary Ellen Bartley; 21, Reuters; 22, Archivo Iconografico, S.A; 23, Richard Cummins / Getty Images: title page, 4, Mike Brinson, The Image Bank; cover, 14, Ray Kachatorian, Taxi; 17, Mel Yates, Stone / Alamy: 9, Profimedia.CZ s.r.o / Wayland picture library: 7, 11.

Library of Congress Cataloging-in-Publication Data

Pirotta, Saviour.
  Christmas / Saviour Pirotta.
     p. cm. -- (We love holidays)
  Includes index.
  ISBN - 13: 978-1-4042-3704-9 (library binding)
  ISBN - 10: 1-4042-3704-6 (library binding)
  1. Christmas--Juvenile literature. I. Title.
  BV45.P57 2007
  263'.915--dc22
                                    2006026794

Manufactured in China

Contents

Merry Christmas, everyone

Christmas is celebrated on December 25th. Christians believe it is the birthday of **Jesus Christ**.

In some ▶ countries, it gets very cold at Christmas.

4

Christians and many other people celebrate Christmas with great happiness and give each other presents.

Families get together to celebrate. ◀

5

Away in a manger

Christians believe Jesus Christ is the son of God. He taught people how to live better lives, and how to love God and one another.

It is said that a cow and a donkey kept baby Jesus warm with their breath.
▼

Children act out the story of Jesus's birth, called the **Nativity**. ◄

Jesus was born in a **stable** in the little town of Bethlehem around two thousand years ago.

Deck the halls

Christians call the weeks before Christmas **Advent**. In churches and homes, statues of Jesus Christ and his parents are placed in mangers. They are surrounded by figures of sheep, **shepherds,** and **angels**.

Children in Bolivia collect small figures to put in their mangers. ▼

Before Christmas, there is special food to buy, cards to send, decorations to hang, and presents to wrap.

Some people light a special candle every Sunday during Advent.

◄

Oh Christmas tree, Oh Christmas tree

Some people decorate the trees in their yard too. ▼

The tree is the most popular Christmas decoration in the world. A long time ago, people made all their own decorations to put on their trees.

Today, we
buy most of our
decorations from
stores. There are
lots of different
kinds to choose!

Wreaths with
bows, holly,
and mistletoe
are hung on
the doors
and walls.
◀

11

Peace on Earth

Knock! Knock! On Christmas Eve carolers might come to your door to sing you a carol.

Carolers like these sing songs about the birth of Jesus and what it means to Christians.
▼

Carols are special songs we sing at
Christmas. They are sung in church
too, especially at **Midnight Mass**.

Down the chimney

Christmas is a time for sharing. People send each other cards and exchange gifts. Children wait for Santa Claus to bring them presents.

What will you find in your stocking on Christmas morning? ▶

In olden days in Italy, children who had been naughty only got a lump of coal in their stocking.

In Hawaii, Santa Claus travels on a boat. ◀

christmas is a treat

All over the world, people celebrate Christmas with a magnificent feast. In some countries, like England and the United States, they serve roast turkey.

Russians eat roast goose like this one, or roast pork for Christmas.
▼

Brazilians like to have colored rice with their turkey. Italians eat a special cake called panettone for dessert after Christmas dinner.

Some families play special games and wear party hats at Christmas dinner.
◀

Boxing Day

In England, the day after Christmas is called Boxing Day because it was the day when rich people gave their **servants** a present. It came in a box.

Today, people eat Christmas Day leftovers, like these turkey sandwiches, on Boxing Day.

DID YOU KNOW?

Coins found in a Christmas pudding made of suet, sultanas, and sugar bring good luck!

This man is helping the poor by preparing free Christmas meals for **homeless** people.

The Christmas holidays are an especially good time to think about doing things for others.

A Happy New Year

In a lot of countries, celebrating the new year has become a part of the holiday season. Parties are organized so that people can wish each other good luck for the year ahead.

▶ Portuguese children eat twelve grapes as the clock strikes the New Year.

DID YOU KNOW?

On New Year's Eve, some Italians throw their old furniture out of the window. "Out with the old and in with the new!" they say.

Happy New Year!

We three kings

In many countries January 6th is a day of great celebration. People remember the day when the three kings brought their gifts to Jesus. Some call it "Epiphany." Others know it as "The Day of the Kings."

The three kings brought gifts of gold, **frankincense**, and myrrh. ▼

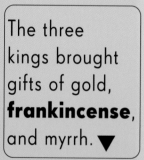

The next day, many people start putting away the decorations. Christmas is over. But we'll celebrate it again next year.

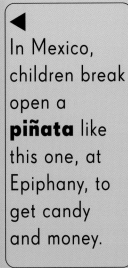

◄
In Mexico, children break open a **piñata** like this one, at Epiphany, to get candy and money.

Index

Glossary

Advent the four weeks leading up to Christmas

angels messengers from God

frankincense / myrrh types of tree gum that make a sweet smell when burned

homeless when a person has nowhere to live

Jesus Christ the person who started the Christian religion

Midnight Mass a church service held on Christmas Eve at midnight

Nativity the story of the birth of Jesus Christ

piñata a cardboard figure that Mexicans break open to find sweets and money

servants people who cook and clean for someone else

shepherd a person who looks after sheep

stable a building where horses are kept